MY ADVENT CALENDAR

Each day of Advent, beginning on December 1, find and color the shape for that day. Then look on the next page to find the message for you from God's Word for that day. On December 25, after all the shapes have been colored in, you may remove this page from the booklet and hang it in your room at home.

Quotes for the day

Find the quote of the day for each day of Advent.

December 1: God saves us

December 2: Wolf and lamb together

December 3: He's prince of peace

December 4: You'll see great light

December 5: Rejoice!

December 6: God loves the poor

December 7: Thank you, Lord!

December 8: Trust in God

December 9: Fill in the valleys

December 10: Make paths straight

December 11: The king is coming

December 12: Come, Lord Jesus!

December 13: The blind will see

December 14: Sing for joy

December 15: Hail Mary!

December 16: Holy is God's name

December 17: God feeds the hungry

December 18: Elizabeth had a son

December 19: Blessed be God!

December 20: Bethlehem, city of David

December 21: No room in the inn

December 22: Shepherds in the field

December 23: You'll find a child

December 24: Mary gave birth

December 25: JESUS

Advent 2000 for Children

Fun Activities, Prayers and Stories

Alison Berger

Illustrated by Holly Bewlay

MY ADVENT JOURNEY

As you travel through Advent, you will meet six special people in the gospel readings. Each week find the figure(s) for that Sunday, trace it (or ask an adult to make a copy for you), color it, cut it out, and paste it onto the outline on this page. Ask your teacher or parent to tell you more about that person.

The six special people are:

Isaiah
Luke
John the Baptist
Elizabeth
Joseph
Mary

Twenty-Third Publications/Bayard, 185 Willow Street, P.O. Box 180, Mystic, CT 06355, (860) 536-2611, (800) 321-0411.
© Copyright 2000 Alison Berger. All rights reserved. No part of this publication may be reproduced in any manner without prior written permission of the publisher. Write to the Permissions Editor. ISBN: 1-58595-123-4. Printed in the U.S.A.

FIRST SUNDAY OF ADVENT

"Watch for me, for I am coming soon." (Luke 21:25–28)

FAMILY TIME
The Gospel for Me

Jesus tells us that if we want his love to fill our hearts, we need to trust him and to pray. Are there things you are worried about or afraid of? Write them on a piece of paper. Invite all your family to do this, too. Then, either when you light your Advent wreath candle or at meal time, put the pieces of paper in a bowl and say this prayer together:

"Jesus, we trust you to take care of us. Help us love you more and more. Amen."

Activity Time

To remind you of today's gospel and to celebrate Jesus' love for us, make a sun and star pinwheel. **Ask an adult to help you.**

You will need: a pencil, a piece of white or light colored construction paper (5"x 5"), a yellow marker, a penny, scissors, a thumb-tack, and an unsharpened pencil with an eraser.

1. Draw yellow stars and suns on both sides of the paper.

2. Take the penny and trace a circle in the middle of the paper. Draw a line from each corner to the edge of the middle circle (Fig. 1). Then cut along the four lines, stopping at the edge of the center circle (Fig. 2).

3. Bring the right corner of each section into the middle (Fig. 3). Put the thumbtack through the four corners, then through the center of the circle (Fig. 4).

4. Push the thumbtack with the pinwheel attached into the eraser of the unsharp-ened pencil. Make sure the thumbtack doesn't stick through the other side.

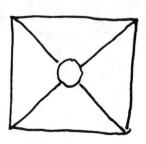

Fig. 1

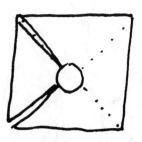

Fig. 2

Fig. 3

Fig. 4

Prayer

Come into our hearts, Lord Jesus.

Luke

It is Luke's gospel that we are reading this Advent.

SECOND SUNDAY OF ADVENT

"Prepare the way of the Lord." (Luke 3:1–6)

PICTURE THE STORY

Find your way through the hills and valleys to the Jordan River where John is preaching.

FAMILY TIME
The Gospel for Me

In Jesus' time when an important person came to visit, the people in the town filled in the holes in the road (remember there weren't any cars or planes). They cleared the way to make the road smooth and clean.

What can you and your family do to welcome Jesus? Perhaps shovel or clean up the yard of an elderly or sick neighbor? Pray more often together as a family? Resolve to be kinder and more helpful to one another? Take part in a community service activity? During your family Advent wreath ceremony or at meal time, ask God to bless you.

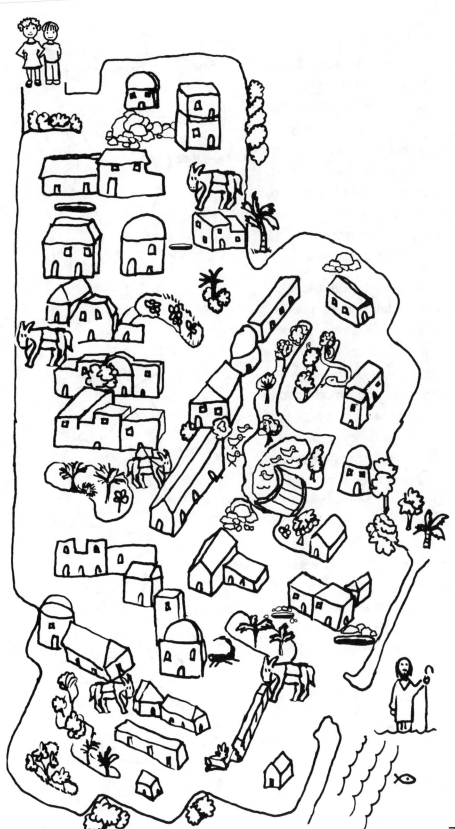

SECOND SUNDAY OF ADVENT

Activity Time

Make beanbag gifts. You will need a piece of felt large enough to trace a dinner plate (approximately 10") and a few small scraps of colored felt, glue, ribbon, popcorn kernels (unpopped; dried beans or rice will also work), and scissors. **Ask an adult to help you.**

1. Trace the dinner plate onto the felt and then cut out the circle. Draw a shape on the felt. It could be an egg, a cross, a fish, a frog—use your imagination!
2. Use the scraps of felt to decorate the figure or to make eyes, noses, or tails.
3. Place the felt circle face down in an empty bowl. Pour about a cup of popcorn kernels onto the felt circle.
4. Gather the outer edges together, securing with a strong rubber band, then a pretty ribbon. You can sell the beanbags at a parish craft show and give the money to those in need. Or give the beanbags to the St. Vincent de Paul Society or a food pantry to use as gifts for needy children.

Alternate Activity

Make a bookmark gift. You'll need a piece of construction paper 2" wide and 5" long, glue, markers, and magazine or greeting card cutouts. Glue a picture to the top half of the bookmark (scenery, a flower, or an animal). Then write a short prayer or a happy thought below the picture. Give the bookmark gifts to some elderly people in your parish.

Isaiah

Isaiah was a prophet who told about the coming of the Messiah.

THIRD SUNDAY OF ADVENT

"I baptize you with water but one who is more powerful than I is coming."

(Luke 3:10–18)

PICTURE THE STORY

Look for the hidden pictures and color them in: boat, bird, fish, shell, and cross. What is happening in the picture?

FAMILY TIME
The Gospel for Me

John was a prophet, the cousin of Jesus. With his words and example he helped people welcome Jesus.

How can you and your family witness to Jesus, that is, show what a difference Jesus' love makes in your life? By being honest, forgiving, unselfish, respectful of others and their property.

Decide together on two ways you as a family can be witnesses this week. Pray about this during your family Advent wreath ceremony or at meal time.

THIRD SUNDAY OF ADVENT

Activity Time

Make your own WWJD (What would Jesus do?) paper weight. You will need a small paint brush and acrylic paints.

Find a smooth rock and clean it. Then use the paint brush to draw the letters WWJD on the rock. You can decorate the rock with pictures of flowers, animals, space ships, or any of your own favorite things. When you have to make a choice about something, look at the rock and ask: What would Jesus do?

(Alternate activity: Make a poster. Draw the letters WWJD on a large piece of paper, then decorate the poster with designs, pictures, or magazine cutouts.)

Prayer

Jesus, help me to treat others as you would.

John the Baptist

John prepared the way for Jesus.

FOURTH SUNDAY OF ADVENT

"Blessed are you, Mary, and blessed is your baby." (Luke 1:39–45)

PICTURE THE STORY

Color the stained glass window by using the color key. What is happening in the picture?

Color Key:

1 = Light Blue (or color lightly with the Blue crayon)
2 = Orange
3 = Green
4 = Dark Blue
5 = Purple
6 = Pink (or color lightly with the Red crayon)
7 = Red
8 = Yellow
9 = Brown

FAMILY TIME
The Gospel for Me

Elizabeth was happy when Mary came to visit. Mary was happy because God is so good.

How often do you say "thank you" to God, to your family and friends, for the good things you receive? Make a list—and ask each member of your family to make a list—of all the things you can be happy about. Place your lists near the Advent wreath or on the table at meal time. Say a prayer of thanks to God.

FOURTH SUNDAY OF ADVENT

Activity Time

The rosary is a special prayer to Jesus and Mary. Make a rosary bracelet. You will need 11 plastic beads with large holes, and a piece of thin ribbon, twine, or plastic cord about 5" long (long enough to fit around your wrist with an inch or two to spare).
Ask an adult to help you.

String ten (10) of the beads together on the ribbon, twine, or cord, then make a knot after the 10th bead. String the last bead, then make another knot. Tie the ends of the twine together.

Let your rosary bracelet remind you to pray to Jesus and Mary during the day. You can use the prayer on this page.

(Alternative activity: Instead of making a rosary bracelet, draw one.)

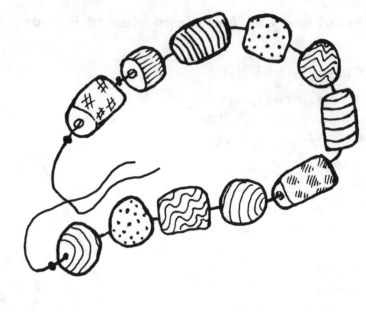

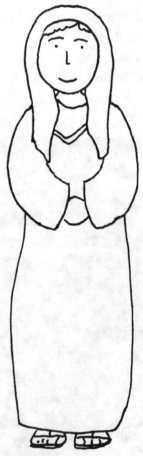

Prayer

Rejoice, Mary! You are full of grace. Blessed is the fruit of your womb, Jesus.

Mary
Mary is the Mother of Jesus, the Mother of God.

Elizabeth
Elizabeth was Mary's cousin and the mother of John the Baptist

CHRISTMAS NOVENA

During the nine days before Christmas we prepare in an even more special way for Jesus' birth. Here are prayers you can say and things you can do for each day.

December 16
Come, Jesus, free us from our sins.
Ask forgiveness.

December 17
Jesus, teach us how to follow you.
Read a gospel story with your family.

December 18
Come and save us, Lord.
Make a visit to church.

December 19
Jesus, help us show our love for you.
Do a secret act of kindness for someone.

December 20
Jesus, help the poor and the homeless.
Give time or money to help the poor.

December 21
Jesus, save people who are treated unfairly.
Be respectful of every person and their property.

December 22
Come, Jesus, bring us your peace.
Pray for peace in the world.

December 23
Jesus, be with us and our families.
Plan some special family time this Christmas season.

CHRISTMAS EVE

"Joseph took Mary to be his wife.... She had a son whom he named Jesus."
(Matthew 1:1–25)

Activity Time

Connect the dots and color the picture.

Prayer

Come, Jesus, stay with us.

Joseph

Joseph was Mary's husband.

CHRISTMAS DAY

"Today the Savior is born." (Luke 2:11)

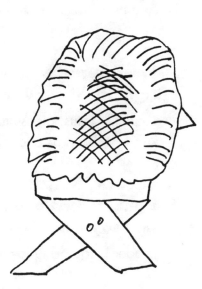

Activity Time

Color the figures. Cut them out and paste them onto a piece of posterboard or construction paper to make your own Nativity scene.

Prayer

Glory to God and peace to all God's people.

Advent Wreath Ceremony

The Advent wreath is a wonderful tradition for the home. If you don't have an Advent wreath, your family can make one. Make a circle out of wire, then use string or twine to attach evergreen branches to the wire. You will also need four candles (three purple or dark blue and one pink; or three white and one pink) with holders. On each Sunday of Advent, the family gathers around the Advent wreath to light the candle(s) and pray together.

First Sunday of Advent
Light the first purple candle and say this prayer together:

Leader   Jesus, please take care of us. May we love you more and more.
All   Bless us and all your people. Amen.

Second Sunday of Advent
Light the first and second purple candles and say this prayer together:

Leader   You bring joy to us, Jesus. Let us bring joy to others.
All   Bless us and all your people. Amen.

Third Sunday of Advent
Light two purple candles and the pink candle and say this prayer together:

Leader   We praise and bless you, Jesus, for your goodness to us. Help us to treat others as you would.
All   Bless us and all your people. Amen.

Fourth Sunday of Advent
Light all four candles and pray together:

Leader   Mary, help us learn from your example to be thankful for all the gifts we receive from God, especially the gift of Jesus.
All   Bless us and all your people. Amen.

VERITAS
·99

TWENTY-THIRD PUBLICATIONS
BAYARD PO BOX 180 · MYSTIC, CT 06355
1-800-321-0411 · FAX: 1-800-572-0788 · E-MAIL: ttpubs@aol.com

9 781585 951239